EXCEL 2016

A step-by-step guide beginner's guide to get you started with

Excel 2016

Table of Contents

INTRODUCTION

Microsoft Excel 2016 makes it possible to analyze, manage, and share information in more ways than ever before, helping you make better, smarter decisions. New analysis and visualization tools help you track and highlight Important data trends. You can even upload your files to the Web and work simultaneously with others online. Whether you're producing financial reports or managing personal expenses, Excel gives you more efficiency and flexibility to accomplish your goals.

The old 80/20 rule for software—that 80% of a program's users use only 20% of a program's features—doesn't apply to Microsoft Excel. Instead, this program probably operates under what could be called the 95/5 rule: Ninety-five percent of Excel users use a mere 5% of the program's power. On the other hand, most people know that they could be getting more out of Excel if they could only get a leg up on building formulas and using functions.

Unfortunately, this side of Excel appears complex and intimidating to the uninitiated, shrouded as it is in the mysteries of mathematics, finance, and impenetrable spreadsheet jargon.

If this sounds like the situation you find yourself in, and if you're a businessperson who needs to use Excel as an everyday part of your job, you've come to the right book. In Excel 2016 Formulas and Functions, I demystify the building of worksheet formulas and present the most useful of Excel's many functions in an accessible, jargon-free way. This book not only takes you through Excel's intermediate and advanced formula-building features but also tells you why these features are useful to you and shows you how to use them in everyday situations and real-world models. This book does all this with nononsense, step-by-step tutorials and lots of practical, useful examples aimed directly at business users.

Even if you've never been able to get Excel to do much beyond storing data and adding a couple of numbers, you'll find this book to your liking. I show you how to build useful, powerful formulas from the ground up, so no experience with Excel formulas and functions is necessary.

PART 1

C1

EXCEL INTERFACE

Let's start with what we mean by the User Interface? Well, this is the part of the software (in this case Excel) that is displayed on the screen of whatever device you are using (laptop, desktop, tablet, phone, you get the idea).

Usually, the User Interface displays all the menus and buttons you click to interact with the functions and features of the software your using. Microsoft refers to these functions and features as Commands, so, from this point forwards so will we.

The User Interface also generally updates and displays the changes that come about as a result of your interactions with the software (Excel). The User Interface can also display messages to the User (you), that might be important.

We'll refer to the User Interface as the UI from now on.

If you've ever used any Microsoft Office software (Word, Excel, PowerPoint, Outlook, etc) over the past few years, you've probably noticed that the UI's look similar.

The Excel UI is broken down into the following regions, Quick Access Toolbar, Ribbon including Ribbon Tabs, Formula Bar, Worksheet Grid, Worksheet Tabs and Status Bar.

Quick Access Toolbar

let's start at the top with the Quick Access Toolbar. In this area of the UI, you'll find some frequently used Commands that can be accessed at almost anytime when using Excel. The Quick Access Toolbar can be customized to add almost any Excel Command.

You'll also find the Filename, OneDrive account setting (and SharePoint account setting) and File Display commands icons such as Minimize, Maximize and Close.

Ribbon and Ribbon Tabs

The Ribbon is where most of the Commands of Excel can be accessed. The Excel Commands are grouped together and can be accessed by clicking the Ribbon Tabs. The Ribbon Tabs are named such as Home, Insert, Page Layout, etc. The Tab names give an indication of the Commands that can be accessed when that particular Tab is clicked.

Formula Bar

Now for the Formula Bar. The Formula Bar has one main purpose, the editing (adding, deleting and updating) of Cell Content. Editing Cell Content can be done by selecting a Cell in the Worksheet Grid and then typing into the Cell Content section of the right-hand side of the Formula Bar.

On the left-hand side of the Formula Bar, you'll see information about the currently selected Cell(s). Generally, when you type into the Formula Bar, it is the currently active Cell that the content will be entered into. However, this can vary, if you drag select a range of cells, then this area will display the number of Rows and Columns in the range that has been selected.

Between the Cell Reference information on the left-hand side of the Formula Bar, and the cell contents on the right-hand side of the Formula Bar, you will see three Command buttons.

The Tick and Cross are enabled when there is Cell Content. You click the Tick to accept the Cell Content, or, click the Cross to delete it. The Third Command button, function (fx) is used to enter formulas.

Worksheet Grid

The Worksheet Grid is the largest part of the Excel UI. It is made up of Cells, arranged in Rows and Columns. The Worksheet Grid is usually where most of the action is. Displaying the data and information in cells that make up the Worksheet.

The Rows are identified using numbers on the left-hand side. Starting at the top of the page and moving downwards using whole numbers, 1, 2, 3, etc. The Columns are identified using letters of the Alphabet across the top of the page, starting at the left-hand side and moving across to the right, A, B, C, etc.

Because we can have more Columns than there are letters of the Alphabet, Excel adds an additional letter to the beginning of the Column when we run out of letters of the Alphabet. For example, Column names could look like X, Y, Z, AA, AB, AC and so on.

Every Cell in the Worksheet Grid is identified by a Cell Reference. The Cell Reference is a combination of the Column and Row identifiers. For example, cell O11, C3, D7, AA14, etc.

The currently active and selected Cell is highlighted by a border around it. Also, the Row and Column headings that make up the Cell Reference of the active cell will be a slightly different color to the other Row and Column headings.

Worksheet Tabs

The Worksheet Tabs region is a fairly straight forward region. An Excel file, sometimes referred to as a Workbook, can be made up of several Worksheets. To navigate between the Worksheets just click the relevant Worksheet Tab, and that Worksheet is displayed in the Worksheet Grid area.

A couple of points worth noting about the Worksheet Tabs region. Firstly, the Worksheet that is currently being displayed is highlighted by a bolder Worksheet Tab than the other Worksheet Tabs. Secondly, a new Worksheet can be added by clicking the Tab with the plus (+) symbol.

Status Bar

The Status Bar. The Status Bar is often overlooked which is a shame because it can be very useful. The Status Bar displays information telling you what Excel is currently doing and displays information about the currently selected Cells.

This information relates to a range of Cells containing numbers that have been selected in the Worksheet Grid. This information can change depending on the type of data in the Cell(s) that have been selected.

It also allows you to access a few Excel Commands, such as adjusting the Zoom Level of the Worksheet Grid, and selecting different View types.

What is new in Excel 2016?

This chapter provides a brief look at some of the changes you will find in Excel 2016. Those changes include the new look of Excel and new capabilities that enable you to better protect, share, save, and edit your worksheet. After reading this chapter, you will understand the new tools and features that you can use to create and share professional spreadsheets with ease.

Slightly New Look

Excel 2016 still has a simplified and clean look to make navigating through various commands easy which in turn will make you more efficient. This new look also includes updated Templates that will do much of the formatting for you. When opening PowerPoint, you are immediately presented with template options. Choosing a template sets the ground work and all you need to do is enter your information. The colors may have changed but the user-friendly platform stays the same.

Tell Me

The "Tell Me" feature is a brand new for Microsoft Office 2016 and is located at the end of the ribbon tabs. Sometimes it can be tricky to remember where commands reside the ribbon, especially if you don't use them often.

The "Tell Me" feature acts as a search bar where you can type in what you are looking for and Word will give you a list of commands to choose from. "Tell Me" saves you from searching through the many ribbon tabs and directs you to the exact command you're searching for.

Share

The new Share button makes it easier than ever to collaborate with others. This button can be found in the upper-right corner, beneath the close button. Once you have saved your document to OneDrive or SharePoint, all you need to do is click the Share button and type in the names of individuals you wish to collaborate with. You can also decide what level of permissions you would like them to have by selecting an option from the drop-down box. Finally, you can include a message with your invite so the recipient knows exactly what you need from them.

Smart Lookup

Smart Lookup is available in all Office 2016 programs, including Word 2016. Think of this new feature as a digital research assistant. It can pull information from the web to enhance your work or assist with unfamiliar content. Simply highlight a word or phrase that you wish to research, then right-click and select Smart Lookup. A pane will appear on the left of the screen with links of information to choose from with more information on the selected text.

Step 1: Highlight word/phrase

Step 2: Right-click the selected text

Step 3: Choose Smart Lookup from the dropdown menu. A pane will appear on the left with web research relating to the selected word or phrase.

C2

CALCULATING WITH EXCEL

When we work in a Worksheet, Excel automatically recalculates all the formulas when we change the values in the Workbook. However, we have the option to recalculate whatever we want, whenever we want. All you have to do is to continue reading.

First, we must select the Formulas tab and from the end right corner of the ribbon named Calculation:

- Calculation Options
- Calculate Now
- Calculate Sheet

If we select the Calculation Options command, the drop down menu will appear where we can choose from the following:

Automatic: All the calculations in the spreadsheet will be done automatically.

Automatic Excepts For Data Tables: All the calculations except for Data Tables in our spreadsheet will be done automatically.

Manual: If we have chosen the Manual command, in order for us to do the calculation in a Formula we must select the Calculate Now command. In order for us to do the calculations in our spreadsheet we must select the Calculate Sheet command.

All we have to do is to click on one of the commands from the Calculation Options drop down menu, and the tick mark will be moved to the left of the command we selected.

Another way in order for us to adjust how our spreadsheet will be calculated is to select the File tab in order to move to backstage view, and from the drop down menu to select the category Options from the left.

Once the category Options is selected the Excel Options dialog box appears where we select the category Formula from the left. Then from the middle of the dialog at the top we notice the area named Calculation Options.

Under this area we have the Workbook Calculation area which is separated from the following commands:

- Automatic

- Automatic Except For Data Tables

- Manual

The commands are the same as the ones that we select from the Calculations area of the Formulas tab and their use is also the same.

UNDERSTANDING FORMULAS AND MAIN WHICH ARE THE MAIN FORMULAS IN EXCEL

All those boxes of numbers aren't going to be very helpful if you can't do anything with them. The formulas and functions in Excel help you do a ton of complex calculations so you can draw meaningful conclusions from your data.

Formulas are the most basic way to do math in Excel. All formulas begin with an = sign. You can then create basic problems using cell labels. For example, in the screenshot above, say I want to see how much the two standalone Wolverine films have made overall in the entire world. I would use the following formula:

=F29+F31

This would add the two numbers together—$373 + $414—to give me a grand global total of $787 million (each cell value represents millions).

Excel also has a ton of pre-made functions to do more complex math for you. For example, say you want to find out how much money the X-Men films have made globally on average in the above spreadsheet. For this, you can use the AVERAGE function. To take the average of all these films, you'd use the following line:

=AVERAGE(F26:F33)

The colon in this line indicates that the AVERAGE function should include the entire range of cells between the first and last cell. So, this function will take the average of every value for an X-Men film in column F.

You can also nest functions within each other. For example, say I want to find out the average user Rotten Tomatoes rating for each X-Men film. The average rating of all the cells in H26 through H33 in the screenshot above ends with three decimal places. Instead, I want to round that number down to a single decimal place. According to Excel's documentation, the ROUND function should be formatted like this:

=ROUND(number, num_digits)

Here, "number" indicates the number I want to round, and "num_digits" represents the number of digits I want to round the number to. In this case, the number I want to round is the result of the AVERAGE function. So, in order to chop those extra decimal points off the average, I'll use the following function:

=ROUND((AVERAGE(H26:H33)),1)

This is what's called a nested function. First, Excel calculates the average of the cells in H26 through H33 (seen in bold above). Then, it uses that average as the number argument in the ROUND function. The 1 at the end of the line indicates that the number should be rounded to one decimal point. So, instead of getting an average rating of 78.875, which is the actual average rating, you see 78.9 in the final sheet.

As you can see, formulas and functions can range from very simple to incredibly complex. These examples just barely scratch the surface of what you can do with formulas and functions. You can check out this guide from the How-To Geek for a deeper dive into what you can do with functions. You can also browse the functions built into Excel and learn how to use them here.

UNDERSTANDING FICTIONS: MATH, DATE, TIME AND SO ON

Time and Date Calculations

When you type a date into Excel, you may never see the underlying serial number, like 40519, but it is there nonetheless. This is a date serial number and it is used in calculating dates.

Excel uses a numbering system with dates beginning with 1 Jan, 1900 as the serial date number of 1 then continued numbering until this day and beyond. For example, a serial number that is 40519 when converted to a date represents 7 Dec, 2010.

When you type a time into a cell in Excel, the underlying value is a fraction, but Excel interprets this as a time serial number and formats the cell accordingly. You can calculate this fraction for any time value during the day by taking the total number of seconds that have passed from midnight until your time value and dividing by 86,400 seconds in a day.

A time value of 6:00PM will show up in Excel as .75

When time and dates are combined, they show up as a serial number with a decimal point. For example: 42446.50 is noon on March 17, 2016.

1. Open the Date and Time sheet.

2. Enter the current date as a fixed date into cell C2 using the Ctrl+; keyboard shortcut

3. Delete the cell contents and replace them with the current date formula =now().

4. In cell D4, use a formula to add 30 days to the invoice date. This will determine the Invoice

Due Date. In this instance type: =B4+30. Autofill the contents down.

5. Next, calculate how old each invoice is by calculating between two dates. In cell E4, type

=C2-B4. The dollar signs are absolute values which lock the cell C2 into the formula.

6. Autofill the formula down.

7. In cell F4, calculate the number of days an invoice is past the deadline. Type =E4-30 and

autofill down.

LOGICAL FUNCTIONS IN EXCEL

Excel logical functions are perhaps the most useful group of Excel functions. Logical functions differ from the other functions because they provide you with a degree of control over the result of a formula.

IF FUNCTION

The IF function is one of the most popular functions in Excel. It allows you to make logical comparisons between a value and what you expect. In its simplest form, the IF function says something like:

If the value in a cell is what you expect (true) – do this. If not – do that.

The IF function has three arguments:

Logical test – Here, we can test to see if the value in a selected cell is what we expect. You could use something like "B7=14" or "B7>12" or "B7<6"

Value_if_true – If the requirements in the logical test are met – if B7 is equal to 14 – then it is said to be true. For this argument you can type text – "True", or "On budget!" Or you could insert a calculation, like B7*2 (If B7 does equal 14, multiply it by 2). Or, if you want Excel to put nothing at all in the cell, type "" (two quotes).

Value_if_false – If the requirements in the logical test are not met – if B7 does not equal 14 – then it is said to be false. You can enter the same instructions here as you did above. Let's say that you type the double quotes here. Then, if B7 does not equal 14, nothing will be displayed in this cell.

The IF Function

The IF function is a logical function that is designed to return one value if a condition you specify evaluates to be TRUE and another value if it evaluates to be FALSE.

Basic Concept: =IF(logical_test, value_if_true, value_if_false)

If the first quarter total is equal to or greater than the 1st quarter quota then the salesman will get the 2% bonus. If not, they get 0.

1. Click on the Bonuses sheet.

2. Select cell G6.

3. Click the Formulas tab on the ribbon.

4. Click the down arrow under Logical.

5. Choose IF.

6. Type what you see in the box below.

7. Using the fill handle, copy the formula down to cell G11.

Changing the "Value if false" Condition to Text

1. Click in cell G6 and click in the Formula bar.

2. Change the 0 to "No Bonus" (you must type the quotation marks).

3. Press Enter and copy the formula down using the fill handle.

3D Formulas

3D formulas typically refer to specific cells across multiple worksheets. This formula is also

sometimes called a "cubed formula". It can, but does not need to, use a function to calculate

across worksheets.

Basic Concept: =Sheet1Name!Cell1Name+ Sheet2Name!Cell2Name

Example1: =SUM('Qtr1:Qtr2'!F5)

1. Click the Summary worksheet.

2. Select cell C5.

3. Type =SUM(.

4. Click on the QTR1 tab.

5. Hold down Shift and click on the QTR2 tab.

6. Click in cell F5, then close the parenthesis in the formula.

7. Press Enter.

8. Drag the formula down.

USING LOGICAL OPERATORS IN YOUR FORMULAS

Excel is very flexible in the way that these logical operators can be used. For example, you can use them to compare two cells, or compare the results of one or more formulas. For example:

=A1=A2

=Λ1−(Λ2*5)

=(A1*10)<=(A2/5)

As these examples suggest, you can type these directly into a cell in Excel and have Excel calculate the results of the formula just as it would do with any formula. With these formulas, Excel will always return either TRUE or FALSE as the result in the cell.

A common use of logical operators is found in Excel's IF function (you can read more about the IF function here). The IF function works like this:

=IF(logical_test,value_if_TRUE,value_if_FALSE)

In essence, the IF function carries out a logical test (the three examples above are all logical tests) and then return the appropriate result depending on whether the result of the test is true or false. For example:

=IF(A1>A2,"Greater than","Less than")

=IF(A1>A2,A1*10%,A1*5%)

However, you don't always need to use an IF formula. Here's a version of this formula that uses a logical operator, and also demonstrates another useful feature of logical operators in general:

=(A1>A2)*(A1*10*)+(A1<=A2)*(A1*5%)

It looks confusing, but in fact it is very logical (excuse the pun). However, it helps to know that in Excel, TRUE is the same as 1, and FALSE is the same as 0.

So, in this example:

If A1>A2 is TRUE, then the formula will multiple (A1*10%) by 1.

Because A1>A2 is TRUE then A1<=A2 is false, so it will then multiply (A1*5%) by 0.

It will then add the results together: (A1*10%)*1 + (A1*5%)*0.

The final result is whatever (A1*10%) equals in the specific example.

Obviously, if A1 is less than A2, then the reverse of this would occur.

Using Multiple Logical Operators

In some cases, you may want to perform more than one comparison as part of your formula. For example:

(Today is Wednesday) and (Sky is Blue)

(Today is Wednesday) or (Sky is Blue)

(Today is Wednesday and (Sky is NOT Blue)

(Today is Wednesday) or (Sky is NOT Blue)

In Excel, you can use one of three logical functions to construct these formulas:

AND

OR

NOT

The AND function works by performing multiple comparison tests and then returning TRUE if all of the tests were true, and FALSE if one or more of the tests were false. Here are a couple of examples:

=AND(A1>A2,A1<A3) (if A1 is greater than A2 AND less than A3, then return TRUE otherwise return FALSE)

IF(AND(A2>A2,A1<A3),"Both are true","At least one is false") (this IF function will return one of the two values depending on whether the AND function returns TRUE or FALSE).

The OR function works in a very similar way to the AND function. However, whereas AND requires that all tests return true, the OR function will return TRUE if only one of the tests return true. For example:

=OR(A1>A2,A1<A3) (if either A1>A2 OR A1>A3 is true, then return TRUE. If neither are true, return FALSE).

=IF(OR(A1>A2,A1<A3),"One or both are true","Neither are true")

It is important to note that the AND and the IF functions can both incorporate up to 255 logical tests (my examples here have only used 2). Regardless of the number of tests you include, the same rules apply as they did in my simple examples.

It is also worth noting that you can combine the AND and OR functions in a single formula. For example:

=AND(OR(A1>A2,A1<A3),A1>A4)

In this example, the AND function will only return TRUE if either (A1>A2 OR A1<A3) AND A1>A4

The final logical function you can use is the NOT function. The NOT function is somewhat self-explanatory - it takes any logical test result and does the opposite. For example:

=(Sky is Blue) - will return TRUE if the sky is blue, and FALSE if the sky is not blue.

=NOT(Sky is Blue) will return FALSE if the sky is blue, and TRUE if the sky is not blue.

Note that this example doesn't care what other colors the sky might be!

Of course, you can use the NOT function with the AND, OR and IF functions:

=NOT(AND(A1>A2,A1<A3)) - if A1>A2 AND A1<A3, then return FALSE

=AND(NOT(A1>A2),A1<A3) - if A1 is NOT >A2 AND A1<A3 then return TRUE.

Note that writing NOT(A1>A2) is another way of writing (A1<=A2). In this simple example, using a NOT function didn't add much value, but in some cases the NOT function can be very handy.

In summary, a lot of what you do in Excel, particularly once you start using IF functions, involves using logical operators. The logical functions, AND, OR and NOT are a great way to extend your use of logical operators to perform more complex calculations.

In column Q we would like Excel to tell us whether a student is passing – or failing the class. If the student scores 70% or better, he/she will pass the class. But, if he/she scores less than 70%, he/she is failing.

1. Make sure that Q5 is your active cell.

2. On the Formulas tab, in the Function Library, find the IF function on the Logical pulldown menu.

C3.

DATA ANALYSIS WITH EXCEL

Sorting Data

Sorting is a common task that allows you to change or customize the order of your spreadsheet data.

For example, you could organize an office birthday list by employee, birthdate, or department, making it easier to find what you're looking for. Custom sorting takes it a step further, giving you the ability to sort multiple levels (such as department first, then birthdate, to group birthdates by department), and more.

To Sort in Alphabetical Order

• Step 1: Select a cell in the column you want to sort by.

• Step 2: Select the Data tab, and locate the Sort and Filter group.

• Step 3: Click the ascending command sort ascending to Sort A to Z, or the descending command sort ascending to Sort Z to A.

• Step 4: The data in the spreadsheet will be organized alphabetically.

To Sort in Numerical Order

• Step 1: Select a cell in the column you want to sort by.

• Step 2: From the Data tab, click the ascending command sort ascending to Sort Smallest to

Largest, or the descending command sort ascending to Sort Largest to Smallest.

• Step 3: The data in the spreadsheet will be organized numerically.

To Sort by Date or Time

• Step 1: Select a cell in the column you want to sort by.

• Step 2: From the Data tab, click the ascending command sort ascending to Sort Oldest to Newest, or the descending command sort ascending to Sort Newest to Oldest.

• Step 3: The data in the spreadsheet will be organized by date or time.

To Sort in the Order of Your Choosing

You can use a Custom List to identify your own sorting order, such as days of the week, or, in this example, t-shirt sizes from smallest to largest (Small, Medium, Large, and X-Large).

• Step 1: From the Data tab, click the Sort command to open the Sort dialog box.

• Step 2: Identify the column you want to Sort by clicking the drop-down arrow in the Column field. In this example, we will choose T-Shirt Size.

• Step 3: Make sure Values is selected in the Sort On field.

• Step 4: Click the drop-down arrow in the Order field, and choose Custom List...

• Step 5: Select NEW LIST, and enter how you want your data sorted in the List entries box. We will sort t-shirt sizes from smallest to largest.

• Step 6: Click Add to save the list, then click OK.

• Step 7: Click OK to close the Sort dialog box and sort your data.

• Step 8: The spreadsheet will be sorted in order of Small, Medium, Large, and X-Large.

To Sort by Cell Color, Font Color, or Cell Icon

• Step 1: From the Data tab, click the Sort command to open the Sort dialog box.

• Step 2: Identify the column you want to Sort by clicking the drop-down arrow in the Column field.

• Step 3: Choose whether you want to sort by Cell Color, Font Color, or Cell Icon in the Sort On field. In this example, we will sort on Font Color.

• Step 4: In the Order field, click the drop-down arrow to choose a color, then decide whether you want it ordered On Top or On Bottom.

• Step 5: Click OK. The data is now sorted by attribute rather than text.

To Add a Level for Sorting Multiple Levels

• Step 1: From the Data tab, click the Sort command to open the Sort dialog box.

• Step 2: Identify the first item you want to Sort by. In this example, we will sort Homeroom # from Smallest to Largest.

• Step 3: Click Add Level to add another item.

• Step 4: Identify the item you want to sort by next. We will sort Last Name from A to Z.

• Step 5: Click OK.

• Step 6: The spreadsheet will be sorted so that homeroom numbers are in order, and within each homeroom, students are listed alphabetically by last name.

Note: Copy Level will add a level by duplicating the one you have selected, and allowing you to modify the sorting criteria. This is useful if you need to sort multiple levels that share some criteria, such as the same Column, Sort On, or Order.

To Change the Sorting Priority

• Step 1: From the Data tab, click the Sort command to open the Custom Sort dialog box.

• Step 2: Select the level you want to reorder.

• Step 3: Use the Move Up or Move

Down arrows. The higher the level is on the list, the higher its priority.

Filtering Data

Filters can be applied in many ways to improve the performance of your worksheet. You can filter text, dates, and numbers. You can even use more than one filter to further narrow down your results.

To Filter Data

In this example, we will filter the contents of an equipment log at a technology company. We will display only the laptops and projectors that are available for check-out.

• Step 1: Begin with a worksheet that identifies each column using a header row.

• Step 2: Select the Data tab, and locate the Sort & Filter group.

• Step 3: Click the Filter command.

• Step 4: Drop-down arrows will appear in the header of each column.

• Step 5: Click the drop-down arrow for the column you would like to filter. In this example, we will filter the Type column to view only certain types of equipment.

• Step 6: The Filter menu appears.

• Step 7: Uncheck the boxes next to the data you don't want to view. (You can uncheck the box next to Select All to quickly uncheck all.)

• Step 8: Check the boxes next to the data you do want to view. In this example, we will check Laptop and Projector to view only those types of equipment.

• Step 9: Click OK. All other data will be filtered, or temporarily hidden. Only laptops and projectors will be visible.

To Add Another Filter

Filters are additive, meaning you can use as many as you need to narrow down your results. In this example, we will work with a spreadsheet that has already been filtered to display only laptops and projectors. Now we will display only laptops and projectors that were checked out during the month of August.

• Step 1: Click the drop-down arrow where you would like to add a filter. In this example, we will add a filter to the Checked Out column to view information by date.

• Step 2: Uncheck the boxes next to the data you don't want to view. Check the boxes next to the data you do want to view. In this example, we will check the box next to August.

• Step 3: Click OK. In addition to the original filter, the new filter will be applied. The worksheet will be narrowed down even further.

To Clear a Filter

• Step 1: Click the drop-down arrow in the column from which you want to clear the filter.

• Step 2: Choose Clear Filter From...

• Step 3: The filter will be cleared from the column. The data that was previously hidden will be on display once again.

Slicer Filter

Slicers make it faster and easier to filter and analyze Tables, Pivot Tables, Pivot Charts, and cube functions. They allow you to focus on one area of data more clearly.

• Step 1: Under PivotTable Tools select the Analyze tab and click on Insert Slicer in the the Filter group.

• Step 2: Check the category or categories that you want to view and click OK.

• Step 3: When you click on specific data in the Slicer your PivotChart will show the information associated with that data.

Timeline Filter

The Timeline filter makes it faster and easier to select time periods to filter PivotTables, Pivot Charts, and cube functions.

• Step 1: Under PivotTable Tools select the Analyze tab and click on Insert Timeline in the Filter group.

• Step 2: Check the category with the dates you want to filter and click OK

• Step 3: Your Date Timeline will appear. You can view it in Years, Quarters, Months, or Days by using the dropdown arrow in the top right corner. Slide the ends of the bar left and right by clicking and dragging to view only a certain span of dates in your PivotTable.

Insert Tab Intermediate

Inserting Charts

Excel workbooks can contain a lot of data, and that data can often be difficult to interpret. For example, where are the highest and lowest values? Are the numbers increasing or decreasing?

The answers to questions like these can become much clearer when the data is represented as a chart.

Excel has many different types of charts, so you can choose one that most effectively represents the data.

To Create a Chart

• Step 1: Select the cells that you want to chart, including the column titles and the row labels. These cells will be the source data for the chart.

• Step 2: Click the Insert tab.

• Step 3: In the Charts group, select the desired chart category (Column, for example).

• Step 4: Select the desired chart type from the drop-down menu (Clustered Column, for example).

• Step 5: The chart will appear in the worksheet.

Recommended Charts

The Recommended Charts button takes a lot of the guess work out of what kind of chart you should use to represent your data by suggesting what type of chart will be the best fit and why.

• Step 1: Select the data that you want to use in your chart.

• Step 2: Under the Insert tab in the Charts group click on the Recommended Charts button.

To Change the Chart Type

• Step 1: From the Design tab, click the Change Chart Type command. A dialog box appears.

• Step 2: Select the desired chart type and click OK.

TRANSFORMING DATA

In 2013, Microsoft released the Power Query plugin for Excel 2010 and 2013 that enabled users to extract, transform and load the data into a workbook or a model. With its increasing popularity, Microsoft integrated the feature completely into Excel 2016/Office 365 and renamed it Get & Transform, which exactly describes its functionality. The old plugin and the corresponding Excel 2016 component are receiving regular updates.

Performed ETL (extract, transform, load) steps are recorded and stored as a query. You can alter the query through the UI or as raw text, and you can refresh, reuse and transport the query. This is possible because the query is stored in a language called M.

Extracting is done by choosing one of the various offered data sources from different kinds of text files over popular databases (not just Microsoft!), web sites (URLs), OData feeds and other services like Dynamics, Azure, SharePoint, SalesForce, Exchange Online and even Active Directory. As a fallback, ODBC is also supported.

The second step transformation is done in the query editor, a window that usually directly pops up after specifying the data source parameter.

Behind the View tab, the Advanced Editor can be launched. It offers transformation directly with the M code.

I would describe M as a functional scripting language that is near the .net framework.

It is fast for processing big amounts of data and offers functions for text manipulation, dates, basic arithmetic calculations, simple conditions and even some advanced data structures like lists.

An advantage over traditional macros, which are based on Visual Basic for Applications (VBA), is that M is neither influenced by the language of the operating system nor the office package.

The third and last step load is triggered by clicking the Close & Load button. The default action transformed data is finally shown in a new Excel sheet.

When handling big amounts of data, the query result can be also stored in a data model and used for further processing.

Power Query/Get & Transform is one of the new BI tools in Excel. There is Power Pivot, Power Maps and Power View.

Power Query/Get & Transform is also part of Microsoft's Power BI. It looks and works exactly the same. M queries can be used in both without modifications.

If you're using Excel 2016, start by choosing the Data tab in the menu ribbon. If you have Excel 2010, you'll find a new tab name, 'Power Query'.

USING PIVOT TABLES TO ANALYSE DATA

Pivot Tables

A pivot table is a special Excel tool that allows you to summarize and explore data interactively.

Table - A collection of data. It was first coined in MS Access. However, it is commonly used in Excel nowadays. A table in Excel has a header and there are no entirely blank rows or columns.

(Example: Home > Format as Table)

Pivot - The ability to alter the perspective of retrieved data.

Pivot Table - The ability to create a brand new table based on existing data for the purpose of viewing, reporting and analyzing data.

Creating a Pivot Table

1. Click on the Performance Appraisals worksheet.

2. Click in a cell within the data range.

Note: No entirely blank rows or columns can exist. There must be a header row for a

PivotTable to work.

3. Click the Insert tab on the ribbon and click the PivotTable button in the Tables group.

4. Accept the defaults, click the OK button.

5. A PivotTable will open in a brand new sheet titled Sheet1 and inserted to the left of the

Performance Appraisals worksheet.

Specifying PivotTable Data

Before creating a PivotTable you must know what you want to analyze. There are three questions you have to ask before proceeding:

- What do you want your column headers to be?
- What do you want your row headers to be?
- What data do you want to analyze?

By understanding the layout, you will have a better perspective on how to create a PivotTable.

1. Click back on the Performance Appraisals sheet and ask participants if it is possible to

determine the average salary for each performance rating.

2. Expand to see if you can group that data by Position and Department as well.

3. Click back on Sheet1.

4. Drag the Performance Rating field down to the Rows area.

5. Drag the Salary over to the Values area.

6. A PivotTable will begin to show the results of the data analysis.

7. Drag the Performance Rating field from the Rows area to the Column area.

8. Drag down Position to the Rows area.

9. Your PivotTable will now show the income for each position separated by Performance

Rating.

Changing a PivotTables Calculation

1. Click the dropdown arrow next to Salary in the PivotTable Fields list.

2. Select Value Field Settings.

3. Change the Summarize value field by: to Average.

4. Click OK.

Creating a PivotChart

1. Select Sheet1 (the PivotTable created based on Performance Appraisals).

2. In the Analyze tab under the PivotTable Tools tab menu, select PivotChart in the Tools

group.

3. Choose the default column chart.

4. Click OK.

5. A new chart is added on top of the data.

6. Remove Position from the Rows area.

7. The chart updates accordingly.

8. Delete the chart.

9. Click on a cell inside the PivotTable.

10. Press the F11 key. This is another way to create a chart. This time a chart is added to a new sheet titled Chart1.

11. Drag Department from the Rows area (known as Axis Fields).

12. Drag Performance Rating from the Legend Fields (Column area) to the Axis Fields (Row

area).

13. Change Sum of Salary to Average.

14. The chart updates.

15. Click back on the PivotTable.

16. Double-click on cell B8 (the 1 rating).

Note: It is only one person listed and that is why the results may be skewed

5. Now, the totals will show the Average of each grouping.

FILTERING AND SORTING A PIVOTTABLE

1. Drag the Department field to the Filters area. This top-level filter allows filtering data by

department only.

2. In cell B1, select Administration from the dropdown list.

3. Click OK.

4. The results are filtered to show just those positions that are part of Administration.

5. In cell B1, click the Select Multiple Items checkbox from the dropdown list.

6. Add Executive to the filter and click OK.

7. In cell B1, click the All checkbox from the dropdown list and click OK. All records are now

displayed.

8. Drag Department from the Filters area to the Rows area. Position it so that it lies above the Position field.

9. The positions are now grouped by department.

10. In cell A4, select Training only from the dropdown list. Click the OK button. All other

records are filtered.

11. Click cell A4 and choose Select All. Click OK. All records are now returned to view.

12. Click cell A4 and select Sort A to Z from the dropdown menu. The departments are now

sorted alphabetically.

13. Click cell D3 and choose Sort Largest to Smallest The Performance Ratings now show

the highest rating first.

PART 2

C4

EXCEL VISUALS

Visual Basic Editor

How to open the VBA environment

You can access the VBA environment in Excel 2016 by opening the Microsoft Visual Basic for Applications window.

First, be sure that the Developer tab is visible in the toolbar in Excel.

The Developer tab is the toolbar that has the buttons to open the VBA editor and create Form/ ActiveX Controls like buttons, checkboxes, etc.

To display the Developer tab, click on File in the menu bar and select Options from the drop down menu.

When the Excel Options window appears, click on the Customize Ribbon option on the left. Click on the Developer checkbox under the list of Main Tabs on the right. Then click on the OK button.

Select the Developer tab from the toolbar at the top of the screen. Then click on the Visual Basic option in the Code group.

Now the Microsoft Visual Basic for Applications editor should appear and you can view your VBA code.

FORMATING WORKSHEETS

Formatting Text

To Change the Font

• Step 1: Select the cells you want to modify.

• Step 2: Click the drop-down arrow next to the font command on the Home tab. The font dropdown menu appears.

• Step 3: Move your mouse over the various fonts. A live preview of the font will appear in the worksheet.

• Step 4: Select the font you want to use.

To Change the Font Size

• Step 1: Select the cells you want to modify.

• Step 2: Click the drop-down arrow next to the font size command on the Home tab. The font size drop-down menu appears.

• Step 3: Move your mouse over the various font sizes. A live preview of the font size will appear in the worksheet.

• Step 4: Select the font size you want to use.

Note: You can also use the Grow Font and Shrink Font commands to change the size.

Use the Bold, Italic, and Underline Commands

• Step 1: Select the cells you want to modify.

• Step 2: Click the Bold (B), Italic (I), or Underline (U) command on the Home tab.

To Change the Font Color

• Step 1: Select the cells you want to modify.

• Step 2: Click the drop-down arrow next to the font color command on the Home tab. The color menu appears.

• Step 3: Move your mouse over the various font colors. A live preview of the color will appear in the worksheet.

• Step 4: Select the font color you want to use.

Note: Your color choices are not limited to the drop-down menu that appears. Select More Colors at the bottom of the menu to access additional color options.

To Add a Fill Color

• Step 1: Select the cells you want to modify.

• Step 2: Click the drop-down arrow next to the fill color command on the Home tab. The color menu appears.

• Step 3: Move your cursor over the various fill colors. A live preview of the color will appear in the worksheet.

• Step 4: Select the fill color you want to use.

To Change Horizontal Text Alignment

• Step 1: Select the cells you want to modify.

• Step 2: Select one of the three horizontal Alignment commands on the Home tab.

o Align Text Left: Aligns text to the left of the cell.

o Center: Aligns text to the center of the cell.

o Align Text Right: Aligns text to the right of the cell.

To Change Vertical Text Alignment

• Step 1: Select the cells you want to modify.

• Step 2: Select one of the three vertical Alignment commands on the Home tab.

o Top Align: Aligns text to the top of the cell.

o Middle Align: Aligns text to the middle of the cell.

o Bottom Align: Aligns text to the bottom of the cell.

USING DATA VISUALISATIONS AND CONDITIONAL FORMATTING

Conditional Formatting

Conditional formatting in Excel enables you to highlight cells with a certain color depending on the cell's value. Using this feature can make analyzing data easier by applying visual styles to the data.

1. Open the Conditional Formatting worksheet.

2. Select the cell range D4:H13.

3. On the Home tab, in the Styles group, click the arrow next to Conditional Formatting and

choose Color Scales.

4. Hover over the color scale icons to see a preview of the data with conditional formatting

applied. In a three-color scale, the top color represents higher values, the middle color

represents medium values, and the bottom color represents lower values.

Exploring Styles and Clearing Formatting

On the Home tab, in the Styles group, click the arrow next to Conditional Formatting and then experiment with the available styles by completing the following:

1. Select cell range I4:I13 and apply a 3 Arrows set in the Icon Set menu.

2. Select cell range D15:H15 and apply a Solid Fill Blue Data Bar.

3. Practice using the Top/Bottom and Highlight Cells Rules on the worksheet.

4. From the Conditional Formatting dropdown menu, hover over Clear Rules, then click

Clear Rules from Entire Sheet.

Using Conditional Formatting to Hide Cells

If you have cell contents and you do not want to be visible, you can use conditional formatting to hide them.

1. Select cells G4 through G13.

2. Choose Conditional Formatting from the Home tab and select New Rule from the dropdown menu.

3. Select the Format only cells that contain option.

4. Choose Cell Value is less than or equal to zero as the criteria.

Click the Format button and change the font color to white. This will give the appearance that the cells that do not meet the criteria are hidden.

USING DATA VISUALISATIONS

This short module introduces some methods for creating effective data visualizations from structured data in Excel 2016 using the "Recommended Charts" and built-in charts features. Some common built-in data visualizations: column, line, pie, bar, area, X Y (scatter), stock, surface, radar, treemap, sunburst, histogram, box & whisker, waterfall, combo, and 3D maps. A number of the data visualizations are available in both 2D and 3D versions. This will introduce the work of creating data visualizations in Excel 2016.

Learners will...

review the basics of the structure of "structured data" and consider how data structure (and data amounts) affects the possible data visualizations conceptualize the core descriptive functions of data visualizations from structured data think about whether data visualizations should be linked to their underlying data tables or not, and also when data visualizations should be direct copied or when they should be rendered as image files explore what to consider when selecting possible data visualizations consider the pros and cons to the "Recommended Charts" feature in Excel 2016.

Module Pretest

1. What are the basic structures of "structured data"? How does data structure affect possible data visualizations? What is the importance of the amount of data being visualized?

2. What are some of the core descriptive functions of data visualizations from structured data?

3. When should data visualizations be linked to their underlying data tables? When shouldn't data visualizations be linked to their underlying data tables? Also, when should data visualizations be represented as copied files vs. image files?'

4. What are important points to consider when selecting possible data visualizations?

5. What are some pros and cons to using the "Recommended Charts" feature in Excel 2016? What are some add-ins to Excel 2016 that enhance the data visualization capabilities of the tool?

Main Contents

1. What are the basic structures of "structured data"? How does data structure affect possible data visualizations? What is the importance of the amount of data being visualized?

"Structured data" refers to data in data tables and worksheets. The typical structure is that variables are labeled in the column headers, and the rows consist of records, with unique identifiers in the row headers down the far left column. The data is "structured" because every piece of information is identified. Every cell has a column header and a row header and so is "labeled". Also, the placement of the data in respective cells enables the study of various interrelationships between the table data. Most software tools used to analyze structured data can identify the basic data types: dates, string data, latitude and longitude, and others.

The "structure" of the data (their columnar order, from left to right; the "type" data format for each column; the proper columnar label) has to be correct in order for a software tool to create a corresponding data visualization. For example, an OHLC chart has to be labeled as open, high, low, and close to properly represent the stock chart data. Without those labels and without proper information in the respective cells, a coherent data visualization will not be possible.

The amount of data in a data visualization is important in several ways. First, a 2D and a 3D space—the x and y axes, or the x, y, and z axes—has limited "real estate" to convey information. While these visualizations can often handle millions of lines of row data, only a few columns of data may be addressed in a clear way. Many data visualizations exist in a context, with surrounding descriptive information. Many data visualizations are part of a data visualization sequence, so the necessary information is conveyed in greater completeness over time. Also, many data visualizations are linked to underlying dataset(s), so access to fuller informational understandings is available.

2. What are some of the core descriptive functions of data visualizations from structured data?

One way to conceptualize data visualizations is as core descriptive functions. Data visualizations communicate the following:

✓   proportionality

✓   frequency (and "intensity")

✓   changes over time

✓   hierarchical relationships (in terms of various groupings and relationships)

✓   descriptive statistics of central tendency and distributions

✓   social relationships

✓   physical –spatial relationships, and others

(For more on this, please see the slideshow "Creating Effective Data Visualizations in Excel: Some Basics" hosted on SlideShare. The slideshow lists various data visualizations linked to the particular core descriptive functions listed above.)

3. When should data visualizations be linked to their underlying data tables? When shouldn't data visualizations be linked to their underlying data tables? Also, when should data visualizations be represented as copied files vs. image files?

By default, a data visualization that is copied out from Excel will be linked to the underlying data. If the underlying data is changed, the data visualization automatically updates to accommodate that change in value in the respective cell (or the changes in formulas or some other change). This connection continues as long as the file are in the same folders and with the same local relationships. If files are moved or links break, then the data visualization will not update.

Copying a data visualization into a slideshow and such for presentation is generally a good idea because the data visualization will be machine (and screen reader-) readable. This means that the data visualization will be more accessible to a broader range of people, including many who have some visual acuity or other perceptual or symbolic processing challenge.

A small downside, though, is that such data tables do not resize very well with proper maintenance of aspect ratio. Also, the data charts have a transparent background (alpha channel), which means that preset page numbers and backgrounds of the receiving documents will show through.

A data chart may be screen-captured and pasted into a receiving document or slideshow. In this case, there is a given non-transparent background.

Resizing with proper aspect ratios is easy. However, the image is not automatically machine readable or screen reader readable. Images have to be annotated with "alt text" with informational equivalency of the original chart.

4. What are important points to consider when selecting possible data visualizations?

The depicted data has to fit the data visualization. There are conventions to different data visualizations. Data visualizations are understood to convey certain types of data, and if the underlying data does not meet the requirements for the data visualization, then researchers should proceed with care and / or caveat their use of a particular visualization for non-conventional data types. For example, histograms are understood to represent continuous data. So if a histogram is used for qualitative and categorical data, that should be noted.

With the ease of data access, and the ease of running statistical analyses over data, and the ease of creating a data visualization, some researchers will blitz through the work and unthinkingly output meaningless (or seriously compromised) data. On the Web are a number of sites and videos that give wrong information on how to output various data visualizations. Such sites make the issue worse. And then, the speed at which people read data visualizations also compounds the problem—of having information mis-shared widely and feeding a sense of alternative facts (untruths).

This is to say that those who would conduct research need to do so in highly professional and careful ways. They need to handle data with care and not introduce error by how they handle data. They need to continue that professional care when structuring data for data visualizations and then outputting and publishing those data visualizations. The speed of technology is impressive and a net positive, but these capabilities benefit researchers who do their homework and take the time needed to do something right. (One additional note: Researchers need to constantly refresh on their statistical understandings to be effective.)

5. What are some pros and cons to using the "Recommended Charts" feature in Excel 2016? What are some add-ins to Excel 2016 that enhance the data visualization capabilities of the tool?

Finally, what are some pros and cons to using the "Recommended Charts" feature in Excel? This feature provides generalist "cognitive scaffolding" for those who are pretty new to data visualizations. This provides a sense of how the highlighted data may be visualized and may help users get into the mental space for creating data visualizations.

What this doesn't do is provide higher-level insights by checking the fit of the data to the data visualization. This doesn't offer deeper insights to other data visualizations that may be possible with the same data. This tool will sometimes glitch and may require a reboot of the software in order for it not to kick up a message that it cannot find data visualizations for a certain set of highlighted data. This is a good tool feature if used properly and with the right expectations.

Finally, for those who are interested in creating more complex data visualizations, they may want to explore add-ins to Excel 2016 from the Office Store, third-party software tools, and other trusted spaces. Add-ins enable complex visualizations like 3D maps, streamgraphs, network graphs, and others. (There is more on this in the slideshow below in the References section.)

Examples

For a wide range of examples, please see the link to the SlideShare slideshow on which this module is based.

How To

The slideshow below in the References area walks users through how to structure data for the various types of data visualizations available in Excel 2016. Because the data is already publicly available and because this module is already quite extensive, readers are asked to download or access the slideshow on SlideShare for their purposes.

Possible Pitfalls

Creating effective data visualizations can be somewhat fraught. This is because data visualizations are by necessity summary data, and they cannot fully represent the underlying dataset. They are also built off selected data, not all the underlying data. What this means is that there has to be mindfulness in the creation of such data visualizations, and the context and data labels and other customization elements should help mitigate some of the potential misunderstandings from the data visualizations. There are a number of free add-ins to Excel 2016 that enable data visualizations of other types—streamsgraphs, networks, and others, to add a wider variety of options for users of this software. Also, properly designed data visualizations will draw viewers in, so that they spend sufficient time to understand the underlying data instead of just making some fast assumptions and thinking that they understand the information.

Releasing underlying datasets? When should data visualizations be linked to underlying data tables? For many researchers in the "hard sciences" conducting research using quantitative data, they are required to share their datasets backing up their research. The requirement may come from the grant funders. For others, publishing datasets is a condition of the publishing entity, which may require "reproducible" research. In these cases, such datasets are released along with the R-code, which enables various queries and dynamic visualizations.

Before datasets are released as stand-alone files, they should be properly cleaned and de-identified. The data should not be re-identifiable. If metadata rides with the dataset, that should also be cleaned off (or should at least not unintentionally or accidentally leak data).

When shouldn't underlying datasets be released? If the researcher lacks legal rights to release the data (such as if he or she or they is / are using others' data), then he or she should not release the data. If third-party data is being used and it is publicly available or open-source, then he or she can link to the data source instead. If the audience receiving the data visualization does not need more data and may lack the sufficient background to understand the data, then it may be better to not release the datasets. (In qualitative research, most datasets contain some private data.

There is not yet a clear way forward on how qualitative research data may be shared constructively given the inherent subjectivity and framing to qualitative research.)

Module Post-Test

1. What are the basic structures of "structured data"? How does data structure affect possible data visualizations? What is the importance of the amount of data being visualized?

2. What are some of the core descriptive functions of data visualizations from structured data?

3. When should data visualizations be linked to their underlying data tables? When shouldn't data visualizations be linked to their underlying data tables? Also, when should data visualizations be represented as copied files vs. image files?'

4. What are important points to consider when selecting possible data visualizations?

5. What are some pros and cons to using the "Recommended Charts" feature in Excel 2016? What are some add-ins to Excel 2016 that enhance the data visualization capabilities of the tool?

GRAPHICS AND DATA USING EXCEL CHARTS

So why do people use Graphs and Charts in Excel? Well usually it's to strengthen a message or sometimes to actually give the message itself. As the saying goes, a picture can paint a thousand words. And very often, particularly with complex data a picture can help people to understand the data without getting too baffled by all of the numbers.

Charts are usually considered more aesthetically pleasing than graphs. Something like a pie chart is used to convey to readers the relative share of a particular segment of the data set with respect to other segments that are available. If instead of the changes in hours worked and annual leaves over 5 years, you want to present the percentage contributions of the different types of tasks that make up a 40 hour work week for employees in your organization then you can definitely insert a pie chart into your spreadsheet for the desired impact.

Graphs in Excel

Graphs represent variations in values of data points over a given duration of time. They are simpler than charts because you are dealing with different data parameters. Comparing and contrasting segments of the same set against one another is more difficult.

So if you are trying to see how the number of hours worked per week and the frequency of annual leaves for employees in your company has fluctuated over the past 5 years, you can create a simple line graph and track the spikes and dips to get a fair idea.

Types of Graphs Available in Excel

Excel offers three varieties of graphs:

Line Graphs: Both 2 dimensional and three dimensional line graphs are available in all the versions of Microsoft Excel. Line graphs are great for showing trends over time. Simultaneously plot more than one data parameter – like employee compensation, average number of hours worked in a week and average number of annual leaves against the same X axis or time.

Column Graphs: Column graphs also help viewers see how parameters change over time. But they can be called "graphs" when only a single data parameter is used. If multiple parameters are called into action, viewers can't really get any insights about how each individual parameter has changed. Average numbers of hours worked in a week and average number of annual leaves when plotted side by side do not provide the same clarity as the Line graph.

Bar Graphs: Bar graphs are very similar to column graphs but here the constant parameter (say time) is assigned to the Y axis and the variables are plotted against the X axis.

How to Make a Graph in Excel

1. Fill the Excel Sheet with Your Data & Assign the Right Data Types

The first step is to actually populate an Excel spreadsheet with the data that you need. If you have imported this data from a different software, then it's probably been compiled in a .csv (comma separated values) formatted document.

If this is the case, use an online CSV to Excel converter like the one here to generate the Excel file or open it in Excel and save the file with an Excel extension.

After converting the file, you still may need to clean up the rows and the columns. It is better to work with a clean spreadsheet so that the Excel graph you're creating is clean and easy to modify or change.

If that doesn't work, you may also need to manually enter the data into the spreadsheet or copy and paste it over before creating the Excel graph.

Excel has two components to its spreadsheets:

✓   The rows that are horizontal and marked with numbers

✓   The columns that are vertical and marked with alphabets

After all the data values have been set and accounted for, make sure that you visit the Number section under the Home tab and assign the right data type to the various columns. If you do not do this, chances are your graphs will not show up right.

For example if column B is measuring time, ensure that you choose the option Time from the drop down menu and assign it to B.

Choose the Type of Excel Graph You Want to Create

This will depend on the type of data you have and the number of different parameters you will be tracking simultaneously.

If you are looking to take note of trends over time then Line graphs are your best bet. This is what we will be using for the purpose of the tutorial.

Let us assume that we are tracking Average Number of Hours Worked/Week/Employee and Average Number of Leaves/Employee/Year against a five year time span.

Highlight The Data Sets That You Want To Use

For a graph to be created, you need to select the different data parameters.

To do this, bring your cursor over the cell marked A. You will see it transform into a tiny arrow pointing downwards. When this happens, click on the cell A and the entire column will be selected.

Repeat the process with columns B and C, pressing the Ctrl (Control) button on Windows or using the Command key with Mac users.

Create the Basic Excel Graph

With the columns selected, visit the Insert tab and choose the option 2D Line Graph.

You will immediately see a graph appear below your data values.

Sometimes if you do not assign the right data type to your columns in the first step, the graph may not show in a way that you want it to. For example, Excel may plot the parameter Average Number of Leaves/Employee/Year along the X axis instead of the Year. In this case, you can use the option Switch Row/Column under the Design tab of Chart Tools to play around with various combinations of X axis and Y axis parameters till you hit on the perfect rendition.

Improve Your Excel Graph with the Chart Tools

To change colors or to change the design of your graph, go to Chart Tools in the Excel header.

You can select from the design, layout and format. Each will change up the look and feel of your Excel graph.

Design: Design allows you to move your graph and re-position it. It gives you the freedom to change the chart type. You can even experiment with different chart layouts. This may conform more to your brand guidelines, your personal style, or your manager's preference.

Layout: This allows you to change the title of the axis, the title of your chart and the position of the legend. You might go with vertical text along the Y axis and horizontal text along the X axis. You can even adjust the grid lines. You have every formatting tool conceivable at your fingertips to improve the look and feel of your graph.

Format: The Format tab allows you to add a border in your chosen width and color around the graph so that it is properly separated from the data points that are filled in the rows and columns.

And there you have it. An accurate visual representation of the data that you have imported or entered manually to help your team members and stakeholders better engage with the information and utilize it to create strategies or be more aware of all the constraints while taking decisions!

Challenges with Making a Graph In Excel

When manipulating simple data sets, you can create a graph fairly easily.

But when you start adding in several types of data with multiple parameters, then there will be glitches. Here are some of the challenges that you're going to have:

Data sorting can be problematic when creating graphs. Online tutorials might recommend data sorting to make your "charts" look more aesthetically appealing. But beware of when the X axis is a time-based parameter! Sorting data values by magnitude may mess up the flow of the graph because the dates are sorted randomly. You may not be able to spot the trends very well.

You may forget to remove duplicates. This is especially true if you have imported the data from a third party application. Generally this type of information is not filtered of redundancies. And you might end up corrupting the integrity of your information if duplicates sneak into your pictorial representation of trends. When working with copious volumes of data, it is best to use the Remove Duplicates option on your rows.

Creating graphs in Excel doesn't have to be overly complex, but, much like with creating Gantt charts in Excel, there can be some easier tools to help you do it. If you're trying to create graphs for workloads, budget allocations or monitoring projects, check out project management software instead.

Many of those functions are automated and without the manual data entry. And you won't be left wondering about who has the latest data sets. Most project management solutions, like Workzone, have file sharing and some visualization capabilities built in.

C5

USING 3D MAPS

Added as Power View to Excel 2013, 3D Maps is the current incarnation in Excel 2016. As its name implies, 3D Maps adds three-dimensional visualization.

Did you know there is a hidden gem in the Insert tab of your Excel ribbon?

Built-in to Excel 2016, 3D Maps gives you the power to create a truly insightful business intelligence tool. To get started, all you need is a dataset with location information. You will find 3D Maps by clicking the Insert tab, and under 3D Map, click Open 3D Maps.

Excel will give you options to display your data on a map in a full 3D rendering. Your data is presented in "Tours", which are made up of

"Scenes." Each scene is a visual representation of your data and can be animated and interactive.

It is easy to change the way your data is presented. Through the use of a flat map or globe display options, you can use various themes that drive the color of your map background elements. When manipulating how your data is displayed, the experience is akin to the pivot tables all us Excel buffs are familiar with.

You have several different charting options – stacked columns, clustered columns, heat maps and more. To add visual impact to your data presentation, you can also combine charting options with different themes and map views. To add visual impact to your data presentation, place your created scenes in a sequence.

Even with the most organized database, some information and insight are lost if not visually engaging for the reader. With 3D Maps, you can generate a three-dimensional presentation of your data that can have a much larger impact on the data than numbers alone. Imagine being able to visually see changes to data over time and by geographical location.

Before you can begin using 3D Maps, you should make sure that your data contains some sort of geographic information within your tables. The data could contain details as complex as longitudes and latitudes or as simple as a zip code or postal code.

To create a 3D Map

- Open a workbook that contains a table of geographical details.
- Click Insert from the top ribbon.
- Click 3D Map under Tours.
- Click on the tour image, in the Launch 3D Maps popup, to begin editing Click on the tour image to begin editing.

The information in your workbook Is geocoded, courtesy of Bing. 3D Maps will then open with your data presented in the areas listed in your workbook.

Drag the fields from the Field list to the Layer pane as needed. The Field List box, next to the Layer pane on the right.

You can use any presented drop-down arrow in the fields to ensure the data is matched correctly to the right geodata. 3D Maps then works to plot the data on the globe in the areas recorded in your workbook. From this point, you can then create a presentation that can be recorded as a video, or interactive navigation for viewers to delve into.

USING SPARKLINES

Sparklines were introduced in Excel 2010 to be a convenient alternative to charts. Unlike a traditional chart, a sparkline is placed inside a cell, allowing you to easily create many sparklines.

There are three different types of sparklines: Line, Column, and Win/Loss. Line and Column work the same as line and column charts. Win/Loss is similar to Column, except it only shows whether each value is positive or negative, instead of how high or low the values are. All three types can display markers at important points, such as the highest and lowest points, to make them easier to read.

Sparklines are basically charts, so why would you want to use sparklines instead of charts? Sparklines have certain advantages that make them more convenient in many cases. Imagine you have 1000 rows of data. If you place a sparkline on each row, it will be right next to its source data, making it easy to see the relationships between the numbers and the sparkline. If you used a traditional chart, it would need to have 1000 data series to represent all the rows, and you would probably need to do a lot of scrolling to find the relevant data in the worksheet.

Sparklines are ideal for situations where you just want to make the data clearer and more eye-catching, and where you don't need all the features of a full chart. On the other hand, charts are ideal for situations where you want to represent the data in greater detail, and they are often better for comparing different data series.

To Create Sparklines

Generally, you will have one sparkline for each row, but you can create as many as you want in any location you want. Just like with formulas it's usually easiest to create a single sparkline and then use the fill handle to automatically create the sparklines for the remaining rows.

• Step 1: Select the cells that you will need for the first sparkline. In this example, we are creating a sparkline for Kathy Albertson, so we will select her sales data.

• Step 2: Click the Insert tab.

• Step 3: In the Sparklines group, select Line. A dialog box will appear.

• Step 4: Make sure the insertion point is next to Location Range.

• Step 5: Click the cell where you want the sparkline to be. In this example, we'll select the cell to the right of the selected cells.

• Step 6: Click OK. The sparkline will appear in the document.

• Step 7: Click and drag the fill handle downward.

• Step 8: Sparklines will be created for the remaining rows.

To Show Points on the Sparkline

Certain points on the sparkline can be emphasized with markers, or dots, making the sparkline more readable. For example, in a line with a lot of ups and downs, it may be difficult to tell which ones are the highest and lowest points, but if you show the High Point and Low Point, it will be easy to identify them.

• Step 1: Select the sparklines that you want to change. If they are grouped, you only need to select one of them.

• Step 2: Locate the Show group in the Design tab.

• Step 3: Hover over the different checkboxes to see a description of each one.

• Step 4: Check each option that you want to show. The sparklines will update to show the selected options.

To Change the Style

• Step 1: Select the sparklines that you want to change.

• Step 2: Locate the Style group in the Design tab.

• Step 3: Click the More drop-down arrow to show all the available styles and select a style.

• Step 4: Select the Marker Color drop-down to specify points.

• Step 5: The sparklines will update to show the selected style.

To Change the Sparkline Type

• Step 1: Select the sparklines that you want to change.

• Step 2: Locate the Type group in the Design tab.

• Step 3: Select the desired type (Column, for example).

• Step 4: The sparkline will update to reflect the new type.

To Change the Display Range

• Step 1: Select the sparklines that you want to change.

• Step 2: In the Design tab, click the Axis command. A drop-down menu will appear.

• Step 3: Under Vertical Axis Minimum Value Options and Vertical Axis Maximum Value Options, select Same for All Sparklines.

• Step 4: The sparklines will update to reflect the new range.

C6

PRINTING

In previous versions of Excel, there was a Print Preview option that allowed you to preview and modify the workbook before printing. You may have noticed that this feature seems to be gone in Excel 2010. It has not disappeared; it has just been combined with the Print window to create the Print pane, which is in Backstage view.

To View the Print Pane

• Step 1: Click the File tab. This takes you to Backstage view.

• Step 2: Select Print. The Print pane appears, with the print settings on the left and the Print Preview on the right.

To Print Active Sheets

If you have multiple worksheets in your workbook, you will need to decide if you want to print the whole workbook or specific worksheets. Excel gives you the option to Print Active Sheets. A worksheet is considered active if it is selected.

• Step 1: Select the worksheets you want to print. To print multiple worksheets, click on the first worksheet, hold down the Ctrl key, then click on the other worksheets you want to select.

• Step 2: Click the File tab.

• Step 3: Select Print to access the Print pane.

• Step 4: Select Print Active Sheets from the print range drop-down menu.

• Step 5: Click the Print button.

To Print the Entire Workbook

• Step 1: Click the File tab.

• Step 2: Select Print to access the Print pane.

• Step 3: Select Print Entire Workbook from the print range drop-down menu.

• Step 4: Click the Print button.

To Print a Selection, or Set the Print Area

• Step 1: Printing a selection (sometimes called setting the print area) lets you choose which cells to print, as opposed to the entire worksheet.

• Step 2: Select the cells that you want to print.

• Step 3: Click the File tab.

• Step 4: Select Print to access the Print pane.

• Step 5: Select Print Selection from the print range drop-down menu.

• Step 6: You can see what your selection will look like on the page in Print Preview.

• Step 7: Click the Print button.

To Change Page Orientation

Change the page orientation to Portrait to orient the page vertically or Landscape to orient the page horizontally. Portrait is useful for worksheets needing to fit more rows on one page, and Landscape is useful for worksheets needing to fit more columns on one page.

• Step 1: Click the File tab.

• Step 2: Select Print to access the Print pane.

• Step 3: Select either Portrait Orientation or Landscape Orientation from the orientation dropdown menu.

To Fit a Worksheet on One Page

• Step 1: Click the File tab.

• Step 2: Select Print to access the Print pane.

• Step 3: Select Fit Sheet on One Page from the Scaling drop-down menu.

• Step 4: Your worksheet is reduced in size until it fits on one page. Remember that if it is scaled too small it might be difficult to read.

To Modify Margins While in Print Preview

The margins of your worksheet may need to be adjusted to make data fit more comfortably on the printed page. You can adjust the margins in Print Preview.

• Step 1: Click the File tab.

• Step 2: Select Print to access the Print pane.

• Step 3: Click on the Show Margins button. Your margins will appear.

• Step 4: Hover your mouse over one of the margin markers until the double arrow appears.

• Step 5: Click and drag the margin to your desired location.

• Step 6: Release the mouse. The margin is modified.

Printing from the Ribbon

Set Print Area

If you find yourself often printing from the same section of a worksheet you can set a print area for that section. This way, when you print your worksheet only that section will print.

• Step 1: Select the cells you want to print. If you want to set multiple areas hold Ctrl and click the areas you want to print. Each area will print to its own page.

• Step 2: Click the Page Layout tab and in the Page Setup group click Print Area.

• Step 3: Click View and Page Break Preview to see the print area and make sure you have selected what you want.

Add Cells to Print Area

• Step 1: Select the cells that you want to add to the print area.

• Step 2: Click the Page Layout tab and click Print Area in the Page Setup group.

• Step 3: Click Add to Print Area from the drop-down menu.

selected what you want.

Clear Print Area

• Step 1: Click anywhere in your worksheet

• Step 2: Click the Page Layout tab and in the Page Setup group click Print Area.

• Step 3: From the dropdown menu click Clear Print Area.

ONLINE EXCEL

Microsoft's Office Online is a completely free, web-based version of Microsoft Office. This online office suite is clearly competing with Google Docs, but it's also a potential replacement for the desktop version of Office.

We'll compare Office Online to both the desktop version of Microsoft Office and Google Docs to see where it fits. Should you use Office Online instead of Office 2016 or Google Docs?

Office Online vs. Desktop Office

Becausee it's a web application that runs in your browser, Office Online will run on everything, from Linux PCs and Chromebooks to iPads and Android tablets. It doesn't require any special plug-in and works in any popular browser, including Firefox, Chrome, and Safari — not just Internet Explorer.

Office Online saves your documents to your Microsoft OneDrive (formerly known as SkyDrive) storage online. You can use the OneDrive integration in Windows 8.1 or the OneDrive desktop application on previous versions of Windows to sync the documents you create to your computer, getting local copies in Microsoft Office format. Office 2013 saves your documents to OneDrive by default, so Office Online works well as a companion web application. Your documents may already be available in OneDrive.

The web-based version of Office also offers better collaboration features than the desktop-based version of Office does. For example, when you collaborate with other people in the desktop version of Word 2013, only one person can edit the same paragraph at a time. Word Online offers real-time editing that allows multiple people to edit the same paragraph at a time.

Office Online is more limited than Microsoft Office. Microsoft provides Word Online, Excel Online, PowerPoint Online, and OneNote Online. If you depend on other applications, like Microsoft Access, you're out of luck.

These online applications are also simplified and stripped down. While they offer a similar interface to the desktop version of Office, complete with a ribbon, they have fewer features built in. This isn't necessarily a bad thing, as most people don't use all of the features available in the desktop Office apps. Want to do a mail merge or run macros? You can't do that in Office Online, but you probably don't need those features anyway.

Office Online also won't work when you don't have an Internet connection. If you want to edit documents offline, you'll need the desktop version of Office.

Pros: Office Online is completely free, can easily be accessed from any device, and is better for real-time collaboration.

Cons: Office Online only provides a few popular Office applications, doesn't have many of the more advanced features, and only works when you have an Internet connection.

Office Online vs. Google Docs

Google Docs is Google's free, web-based office suite. Office Online is Microsoft's response to the rise of Google Docs.

Office Online and Google Docs are fairly similar at this point. Both are free, web-based applications you run in your browser. Both are simplified, stripped-down experiences that save your files to an online storage service — Microsoft OneDrive or Google Drive. Both have built-in real-time collaboration features. Both offer applications for creating documents, spreadsheets, and presentations. Google Docs also offers applications for creating forms and drawings, but Office Online offers a full-featured note-taking app in OneNote. Each has a few different features the other doesn't have, but they're very similar for average users.

C7

BENEFITS OF USING EXCEL

As the most widely used spread sheet and data management tool in the world, MS Excel provides greater flexibility and compatibility across devices and operating systems. Arranging, analysing and presenting your data with MS Excel has never been easy, whether you are a PC, Mac, iPad®, iPhone®, Android™ tablet, and Android™ phone user.

Other than great flexibility, superior number crunching powers and easy access MS Excel also provide its users many benefits including;

Layout your data

Designed to provide an in depth insight into all your data, Microsoft Office Excel allows you to layout your text data in spreadsheet or workbook format. Excel spreadsheets and workbooks can be used to bring information and data from various files and locations to a single destination, for them to be crunched and analysed on a single file.

Easy to reformat and rearrange data

Format your spreadsheets easily using different colour shades, bold, italics to bring the most important data to the fore. Extremely useful when presenting an array of different numbers relevant to the same topic, such as accounting information including pre tax profit and balance carried forward by the company. Moreover MS Excel allows users to select an appropriate colouring scheme for quick analysis.

Process data and analyse with graphs and charts

Given the right input of data, MS Excel will number crunch and analyse your data for you and summarise them for a better presentation with preview options, giving you the opportunity to select the best method to present your story.

Identify and analyse trends and patterns in large amounts of data

MS Excel makes it easy to identify and analyse patterns in your data spreading up to one million rows and 16,000 columns.

Conditional Formatting

The conditional formatting options in MS Excel helps to change the formatting of a cell, based on the information contained. As an example you can have numbers below thousand in red colour and numbers over thousand in blue.

Sharing and Connectivity

MS Excel allows you to share and collaborate with other members of your project or friends group through Share Point or One Drive. It is as easy as sending every one the link to the same file. Once your MS Excel file is saved on to One Drive you and other members can work together on it in real time.

Love it or hate it, Microsoft Office is still basically the standard when it comes to office suites. Office Online feels much more like Microsoft Office than Google Docs does — right down to the ribbon. More importantly, Office Online saves your documents in Microsoft Office file formats like .docx, .xlsx, and .pptx. Office Online should have better compatibility with Microsoft Office files. When you create a file in Office Online, it should look the same in the desktop version of Microsoft Office. Microsoft knows their own file formats, while Google Docs isn't perfect at dealing with them.

Google Docs works offline, but Office Online always requires an Internet connection. Despite Microsoft's Scroogled advertisements, Google Docs has offline support while Office Online doesn't. Google Docs is compelling if you want to use a free office suite offline as well as online — Microsoft would like you to pay for the desktop version if you'd like to occasionally use it offline.

Pros: Office Online offers native compatibility with Office document formats. It also has a more familiar interface if you're used to modern, ribbonized versions of Office.

Cons: You can't edit documents offline with Office Online.

So, should you use Office Online? Well, that's up to you. If you'd like a completely free version of Office so you don't have to pay Microsoft $9.99 a month, it's a compelling option. On the other hand, you may need the more advanced features in the desktop version of Office. If you're already using Google Docs, you may want to switch for the better office document compatibility — or you may want to start with Google Docs for the offline support. It's up to you.

You should give the different applications here a spin and see which one is best for you. Some people need many of the advanced features in Office, while some people just need the basics.

FINALLY

LEARN TO USE EXCEL AND BOOST YOUR CAREER

If you want to learn to use excel, you will want to read the information in this article. Microsoft Excel is a powerful tool for creating spreadsheets and basic database files, and learning to use it properly can have many benefits for your career. This article explores the basics of how to learn to use excel as well as the benefits you will enjoy once you do. When you have finished reading the information below, you will understand how Excel can boost your career, and know where to go to get more information quickly.

What Is Microsoft Excel?

Excel is a spreadsheet application, which means it creates documents arranged in a row and column pattern, composed of individual points on the grid known as cells. Each cell can contain a piece of information, whether that be a number, some text, or a formula. Cells work together, and their grid arrangement makes it very easy to put together basic accounting and finance models such as budgets. The row and column format of a spreadsheet is also very useful in creating "flat files" or simple database tables that contain multiple fields across the top and up to 65,000 different pieces of data in the rows.

What Benefits Can I Expect if I Learn to Use Excel?

Excel can be used for a variety of different tasks in the workplace. Obviously if you work in the accounting or finance departments of your company, then you probably already know how you will be using Excel. However, because of the easy interface and advanced sorting and filtering capabilities, you may find that there are a lot of ways to get more productivity out of Excel that do not involve just numerical analysis. As you learn the shortcuts and techniques for using Excel most effectively, your productivity will increase dramatically and your boss will be impressed. Having the skills to use Excel will also open up new career options for you, often giving you new job possibilities and the potential for a higher salary.

How Can I Learn to Use Excel Quickly?

There are several options for learning Excel. The cheapest but most difficult is to teach yourself out of a book. There are many books available for less than $100 that offer a comprehensive look at all of the features included in Microsoft Excel, however many people find it hard to learn a hands-on application by just reading about it. Instead, many people opt for the (much more expensive) option of taking a classroom based course. These classes will walk you through using the software and all its features, but will require you to take time off from work and adhere to their schedule. The best way to learn to use Excel is by purchasing a computer based training course on CD. This way, you own the software and can go through the lessons as many times as you like, at your own pace.

As you can see, there are many benefits to learning to use Microsoft Excel. Whether you need advanced training for your career, or just want to expand your options, you will find that learning this powerful business software will set you apart from your coworkers and make you more valuable in the job market.

Thank you for reading this book!